For :

The women.

The seekers.

The feminine.

The thinkers.

The tired.

The weary.

The beloved.

The dreamy.

The romantics.

The hopeful.

The givers.

The grateful.

The helpers.

The lovers.

The quiet.

The faithful.

Hello Darlings - Welcome

So often we get caught up in the busyness of life, that we forget to just stop, take a breath and enjoy the beauty of the moment. The stresses are often so overwhelming that we neglect what we really want or need and we go through our days in autopilot mode. As a result, the things that make us happy often take a back seat and our general wellbeing suffers.

The Peaceful Planner has been thoughtfully designed for any woman who's seeking a little more peace and quiet in her everyday world. This Planner will gently encourage you to look afresh at your life as a whole. By doing this you will be quietly inspired to make small and simple changes that will allow more peace, hope and joy to blossom in your life.

Each Month has a comforting theme and a colouring in drawing to spark a conversation with yourself, encourage more self care and motivate you to explore your own creativity. Woven throughout the pages are soft botanical pen and pencil drawings simply because I love all things floral and wanted to add a touch of feminine beauty.

The words "slow" and "rest" touch something deep in my heart and the still, quiet and creative times in my days are where I have regained my peace and hope.

My hope is that this planner will bless your life in all
sorts of wonderful ways!

"Have I gone mad? I'm afraid so, you're entirely bonkers.
But I'll tell you a secret. All the best people are."

-Alice In Wonderland-

A little bit about me.

I'm a Visual Artist, budding author, believer, grateful wife and Mumma to three gorgeous teenagers. The Peaceful Planner is one of my creative gifts to the world!

I've had the most colourful and exciting journey in life so far. I was born and raised in the beautiful African country of Zimbabwe, and after living in Cape Town South Africa with my young family, for a short time, we now live in Mandurah, Western Australia.

After a long and difficult journey learning to accept and manage Bipolar Affective Disorder, I have found that my peace and passion is when I am creating beautiful art and encouraging others to explore their own creativity. After various stays in different Mental Hospitals, years of counselling and Art Therapy, my journey to recovery and mental health has involved creating a routine and structure with activities that contribute towards keeping me well and happy. This ensures that I'm in the best place to love and support my family and friends and do all the "stuff" in daily life. I know the freedom and healing that comes from being vulnerable, seeking help, showing up and sharing your story. I believe that

> "Art is not always about pretty things, it's about who we are,
> what happened to us and how our lives are affected."
> - Anne Brown-

I believe in keeping it real, and by no means have I got it all together or figured out, I still have my rough patches, low days and challenging moments.

A few other things about me, I'm a lover of coffee, and a chocolate and chocolate cake enthusiast. I adore sunshiney days on the beach with a good magazine; girly days out shopping and afternoon naps are the best; Downton Abbey and Pride and Prejudice are my secret joy and classical music and christmas carols calm me. I have a wicked sense of humour, an infectious loud laugh and always tend to take a joke just a little bit too far. I swim often and this is medicine for my body and soul.

I'm deeply grateful for the abundance of love, laughter, struggle, growth and opportunity this gift we call life has given me.

I know it's exhausting being *fabulous* but life's too short not to be!

With love and laughter Ashleigh Vincent

" The beauty
of life lives inside
the smallest of
moments.....
pay attention. "

Kelly Rae Roberts

The Story of a Botanist and Botanical Artist

I have had so much joy creating the whimsical Botanical drawings throughout this Planner. I am absolutely "in Love" with all things Botanical. There is a beautiful family story that runs through these drawings. My children's great grandfather, Grandpa Tom Corby was a Botanist, a graduate of Gwelph University, Canada. He did further studies at Cambridge University and The University of Trinidad. His life's work was dedicated to agricultural research. He started work in Nigeria in 1938 where his research concerned mainly groundnuts, groundnut pests, and a bit about bee-keeping. He moved to Rhodesia in 1947, and was first engaged in pasture research and then maize. The work with maize was spectacularly successful. Then in the late 1950's he turned his attention to legumes, and continued with that for the rest of his life, a period of over 50 years. This was conducted at Grasslands Research Station, Marandellas, Southern Rhodesia (later Marondera, Zimbabwe).

He lived to be just three months shy of a hundred and in his nineties was still focusing on his research. I was absolutely delighted to be commissioned to do the Botanical Drawings for his last Paper, "The Nitrogen Fixing Properties of Legumes".

As a family we have all his research papers and have wondered between us what to do with them all. After chatting to a dear friend Kate Stagg about all of this, she had the best idea and suggested we scan in portions of his writings along with my drawings and in a sense weave his life's work into mine and see his legacy continue. My vision is to create a Range of Botanical Drawings with his words and then see these translated onto various products such as Limited Edition Prints, Stationery and on this our first product "The Peaceful Planner".

What a privilege for me to add his life's work and research into my art, I think Grandpa Tom would be delighted with this!

Proc. Grassld. Soc. Sth. Afr. (1967), 2, 75-81.

PROGRESS WITH THE LEGUME BACTERIA IN RHODESIA

VORDERING MET DIE PEULPLANTBAKTERIEË IN RHODESIË

H. D. L. CORBY
Grasslands Research Station
Marandellas, Rhodesia

ABSTRACT

Progress during eight years of work in Rhodesia with *Rhizobium* is presented. 370 of the country's 50? known indigenous species of legumes have been examined for nodulation, and all but 13 found to form nodules. A collection of 573 isolates of *Rhizobium*, 221 of them from other countries, has been built u? on a basis of selecting strains for agricultural use. Results of greenhouse tests of nitrogen-fixing power of *Rhizobium*, and of field-tests of selected strains, are given. A factory is producing inoculants at the rate of 9000 units a year. A survey has shown virtual absence of ??? ?lure of these inoculants.

UITTREKSE?

Die vordering wat gemaak is oor 'n tydper? ??????? ???? ??????? ??? ??? skryf. Van die land se 50? bekende inhe???? ??????? ??? ?????? ??? ??? dit gevind dat met die uitsondering v?? ?? ???????. ??? ???? ??? ???? Rhizobium-isolate, 221 waarvan van ander lande?, ?? ?????? ?? ????? ??? gebruik te selekteer. Die resultate van ??? ??? ????? ?? ??? ??? van veldtoetse met uitgesoekte Rhizob??? ??? ????? ?? ??? ??? tree 'n tempo van 9000 eenhede pe? ??? ??? ????? ?? ??? ???? in die veld misluk nie.

INTRODUCTION

The growth of leguminous crops on the sandy granitic soils that comprise m??? of Rhodesia's arable farming are??? notoriously poor, and all attempts at ??? proving it by customary agronomic ???? met with no consistent success. Acc???ingly, attention was turned from the legu?es them selves to the bacteria associated with their roots, and in 1958 the Government established a bacteriological laboratory at the Grasslands Research Station to deal with them. Encouraged by the achievement of this laboratory, the Agricultural Research Council of Central Africa opened a sister laboratory on the same station in 1965, charging it initially with the task of reinforc ing the work in progress. As far as is known there are now the only laboratories in Afri?? ?orth of Pretoria that ?re dealing with *Rhizobium*.

In general, work ?as shown t?at the main cause of poor growth of legum?ous crops on the sandy soils concerne? is lack of appropriate strains of Rhi??? ?nd that

???? ??? ??? ??????? ??? ??? ?????? ?? ????? ??? ???? ? bee? ??? at ?rass?nds with ?? past?re ?egum??, it has n? reached ? ? repor? ?e to ?his Congre?? In the m??? time ? is th?ught that th? more advance? work ?ith th? bacteriology of crop-legume? will ??rve to ?how what can be done, an? this a?count ? it is presented with that i? mind.

NODULAT??? ? RHODESIAN LEGUMES

For its s?? Rhodesia has a wealth ? legumes; in?eed the *Leguminosae*, with 50? known spec??, is the best-represented famil? of the *Sper?atophyta* in the country, th? ??xt larges? family, the *Gramineae*, havin? ??t 413 (W?ld, !665) species. Nineteen ? the twen?-five tribes comprising th? *Leguminos?e* are represented, the notab?? agricultura? exceptions being the *Trifolie?* and the *V?cieae*, which are entirely absen? Further de?ail is given in Table 1.

Peaceful Whispers

Our daily routines can make a huge difference to how healthy, happy, peaceful and productive we are. While the word 'routine' sounds boring, it's essential to creating structure, maintaining meaning and keeping you grounded. Our routines don't have to be set in stone, but rather see these suggestions as peaceful whispers.

Be Quiet

Start each day with a grateful heart in a quiet place in your home. Find time in your day that is 100% yours and as quiet as humanly possible. Have a Journal and pen nearby, and a nice warm cuppa. Set your heart towards your day. Find a daily reading book or devotional, spend time in prayer or meditation and soak up the stillness.

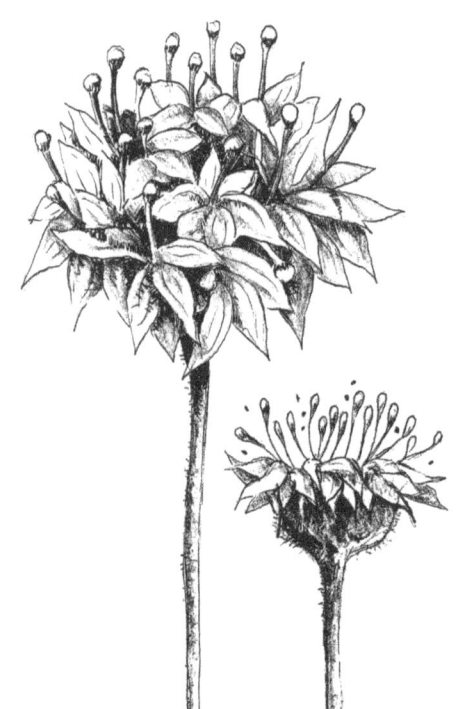

Plan

What do you hope to do and achieve each day, week, month and year? Don't forget it's not just a "to do list". Schedule in your rest and fun times too!

Move

Move your beautiful body, Yes, move it!!

Nourish

Enjoy the wonderful pleasure of eating nutritious, yummy, wholesome food and drinking lots of water. Warming drinks, like tea and coffee are so comforting and to be honest, life would be pointless without chocolate cake.

Reach Out

Foster your friendships and your family relationships. Plan opportunities to have fun together and create memories. Reach out to those in need. Seek to learn from the wise and foster a healthy community around you.

Work

Pursue your craft. Create something. Chase your dreams. Delight in your everyday work; it's a gift!

UnPlug

Take time away from your devices and technology.

Reflect

At the end of the day or week, take time to reflect. What have you learnt, experienced and done? What could you have done differently? What was the best part of your day?

Rest

Make sure you get enough time to rest and relax in your day. Ensure you also get a good night's sleep. If this is something you struggle with, consider creating a routine in the evenings that will help you. A warm bath, cup of camomile tea, no devices in your bedroom and set a time to turn off the lights.

Finding Your Peace

As a human being you are fearfully and wonderfully made. You are a beautiful combination of your Body, Mind and Soul.

Your journey to a more peaceful everyday, comes with the revelation that you actually hold quite a lot of influence over yourself and common sense shows you can work on each of those three areas in your life.

The reality is that this takes planning, effort and perseverance. Take the time to consider how you can nurture each of these areas in your daily life and you will definitely experience more peace and purpose in your everyday. Your self care is essential to your overall happiness.

You will reap a harvest of benefits that will impact your "Body, Mind and Soul" for good!

Body

Your body is the home of your mind and soul. It is the vehicle containing your five senses by which you interact with the physical world around you. Our bodies love nutritious food, lots of water, fresh air, sunshine, laughter, enjoyable movement, soothing touch, hugs and stretches. Our bodies are not ornaments but are the vehicles for our dreams!

Mind

Your mind is found in the amazing organ of your brain. It contains all your thoughts, emotions and your will. It's the area in which you think and reason. It's the home of your intellect, your consciousness and your memories. Your mind holds tremendous potential. Your mind loves truth, knowledge, humour, to learn, to engage in creativity, to work, to be challenged in thought or tasks, to solve puzzles and to create things of beauty. Your mind is pretty awesome!

Soul

Your soul (spirit) is the innermost part of you, through which you experience the deeper things. It's your very essence, the breath of life, it's that still, soft part that enters into prayer and meditation. Your soul loves truth and light, it wants to be known and is the seat of peace.

Considering all of this you can now gently and carefully start finding more peace in your daily routines by making sure you are looking after and nourishing yourself in each of these areas. Your journey will be unique to you, there is no quick prescription it is a daily journey of discovery, learning and experience.

Peaceful Plans

Which ideas take your fancy?

Body

Go for a walk

Gym class

Swim

Enjoy a coffee

Drink lots of water

Yoga class

Pilates

Cycle

Stretch

Join a dance class

Eat something nourishing

Have a massage

Have a facial

Do some gardening

Take a nap

Indulge in a treat

Have a sleep

Mind

Read a good book

Follow a New Blog

Take a course

Write a book

Watch a good movie

Have a meaningful
conversation with
a close friend

Go to the theatre

Enjoy live music

Research something
you're interested in

Watch a documentary

Visit a library

Soul

Create a quiet
cozy space

Keep a journal

Pray

Meditate

Sing an old hymn

Learn some uplifting
verses, quotes
or old wisdom

Choose to be a seeker

Find truth

Ponderings

A few ideas to motivate you to seek your peace...
Ponder these awhile...

Creative Calm

When we use the creative area in our brains, in very simple terms, it actually gives our minds a "rest"...

That is why I have hand-drawn "colouring-in" pages for you to do each month. Take the time to reconnect with your inner creative child, get yourself some nice crayons and enjoy making your pictures beautiful!

Each month you will also find a creative idea waiting for you to think about, it may inspire you to try something new, gather a group of friends and do something together, or take a trip to your local art supply shop and get yourself a sketchbook and some pencils.

I truly believe that everyone is creative in their own way, whether it be painting, sewing, blogging, making your home beautiful, scrapbooking, baking, gardening, songwriting, writing a book, taking photographs, writing poetry, doodling in a sketchbook or creating a new idea board on Pinterest.

Indulge yourself with a creative activity and remember it's about the process not the end product... Enjoy!

" When you Recover or Discover something that nourishes
your soul and brings you joy, care enough about yourself
to make room for it in your life."

-Jean Shinoda Boden-

" The rest notes in the music of our lives, are the places that bring the most magnificent beauty.

Are you filling your days with so much noise that there is no rest in the orchestra of shoulds ?

We are the composers of our everyday.

Stop.
Step out of the traffic.
Breathe.
Notice the steam rising off your hot coffee.

Breathe in deep the rain that stings your skin.

Do nothing.
For a moment.
Nothing.
Rest. "

-Amanda Viviers-

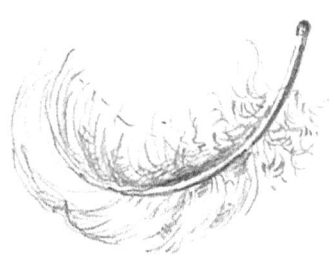

Calm

Kirkia 13 (1): 1988

TYPES OF RHIZOBIAL NODULES AND THEIR DISTRIBUTION AMONG THE LEGUMINOSAE*

H. D. L. CORBY

Department of Botany, University of Zimbabwe

SUMMARY

Calm

Calm... When do you feel Calm?
What or who is calm around you?
Which colours make you feel calm?

Sit outside and listen to the birds,
Put your feet up and close your eyes,
Think of some of the most beautiful places you have been to
That touched your soul and brought a renewed
sense of calm into your world.

"An unhurried sense of time is in itself,
a form of wealth."

-Unknown-

Important Projects

Where you get to focus on the important over the urgent

Think About...	Work on...	Finished!

My three main intentions for this month:

One	Two	Three

Could do list

_____

_____

_____

_____

_____

_____

_____

_____

_____

_____

_____

_____

_____

_____

_____

"Oh, these vast, calm, measureless mountain days, days in
whose light everything seems equally divine, opening a
thousand windows to show us God. "

-John Muir-

This Month

Monday	Tuesday	Wednesday	Thursday

Get Creative...
Start the year by creating a vision board. Choose a big piece of cardboard, a blank canvas or corkboard and gather a series of magazines. Take time to cut out pictures that speak to you about the things you love or aspire to achieve this year. Piece them together in a collage with inspirational quotes and when you are finished, place your board somewhere you will see it every day. It's the perfect way to set your goals and keep you motivated through the days, especially the ones that are tougher than others.

" Beautiful music is the art of the prophets that can calm the agitations of the soul;
it is one of the most magnificent and delightful presents God has given us."

-Martin Luther-

Friday	Saturday	Sunday

Notes and Scribbles...

Calm

Calm

"I go to the ocean to calm down, to reconnect with the creator, to just be happy."
-Nnedi Okorafor-

Monday
_____

Tuesday
_____

Wednesday
_____

Thursday

Friday

Saturday

Sunday

Calm

"Getting stress out of your life takes more than prayer alone.
You must take action to make changes and stop doing whatever is causing the
stress. You can learn to calm down in the way you handle things."
-Joyce Meyer-

Monday

Tuesday

Wednesday

Thursday

Friday

Saturday

Sunday

Calm

"For there is no friend like a sister in calm or stormy weather; To cheer one on the tedious way, to fetch one if one goes astray, to lift one if one totters down, to strengthen whilst one stands."
-Christina Rossetti-

Monday

Tuesday

Wednesday

Thursday

Friday

Saturday

Sunday

Calm

"If I want to calm down, I'll buy some fabric, get a pattern,
shut myself in a room and stay there for days, really happy. At the end of it, you
get a bedspread or some curtains or something to wear - it's lovely."
-Twiggy-

Monday

Tuesday

Wednesday

Thursday

Friday

Saturday

Sunday

Calm

"Affliction is the wholesome soil of virtue, where patience,
honor, sweet humility, and calm fortitude, take root and strongly flourish."
-David Mallet-

Monday
_____

Tuesday
_____

Wednesday
_____

Thursday

Friday

Saturday

Sunday

Reflections

Colour Me In

Peaceful

H. D. L. CORBY

TABLE 2

Root-colour in the Leguminosae

Nodulative status*	Numbers examined			Percentage of records coloured
	Genera	Species	Records	
N	6	17	33	15
N	11	95	72	5
N	8	73	40	14
N	12	41	72	47
N	1	3	4	0
N	22	89	143	14
N	4	4	5	40
A	2	2	5	60
N	64	322	579	
A	2	2	15	
N	1	38	113	10
N	2	2	7	57

Peaceful

Seeking peace is a key to remaining happy in ourselves and in our relationships with others around us.

It's a good idea to check in with ourselves and ask if there is anything keeping us from feeling more at peace, do we need to forgive someone, or say sorry to someone, maybe even ourselves.

Is there a task we've been putting off doing or would it just be a walk out in the fresh air that would renew our sense of peace.

" Being at peace is the ultimate position of power "

-Unknown-

Important Projects

Where you get to focus on the important over the urgent

Think About...	Work on...	Finished!

My three main intentions for this month:

One	Two	Three

Could do list

_____

_____

_____

_____

_____

_____

_____

_____

_____

_____

_____

_____

_____

_____

"Today, soak in what's real and what's real is unhurried.
The ground. The air. The exhale. The planted seed. The shift. The season."

- Victoria Erickson -

This Month

Monday	Tuesday	Wednesday	Thursday

Get Creative...
Go out on an Inspiration walk. Choose a place where you are more likely to find
interesting things to collect, such as a beach, the bush or a beautiful garden

" And so while others miserably pledge themselves to the insatiable pursuit of ambition and brief power, I will be stretched out in the shade singing."

-Fray Luis De Leon-

Friday	Saturday	Sunday

Notes and Scribbles...

Peaceful

Peaceful

"Surfing soothes me, it's always been a kind of Zen experience for me. The ocean is so magnificent, peaceful, and awesome. The rest of the world disappears for me when I'm on a wave."
-Paul Walker-

Monday

Tuesday

Wednesday

Thursday

Friday

Saturday

Sunday

Peaceful

"Cross the meadow and the stream and listen
as the peaceful water brings peace upon your soul."
-Maximillian Degenerez-

Monday

Tuesday

Wednesday

Thursday

Friday

Saturday

Sunday

Peaceful

"The Dove, on silver pinions, winged her peaceful way."
-James Montgomery-

Monday

Tuesday

Wednesday

Thursday

Friday

Saturday

Sunday

Peaceful

"Peace is the result of retraining your mind to process
life as it is rather then how you think it should be."
-Wayne Dyer-

Monday
_____

Tuesday
_____

Wednesday
_____

Thursday

Friday

Saturday

Sunday

Peaceful

"Your life becomes a masterpiece when you learn to master peace"
-Unknown-

Monday

Tuesday

Wednesday

Thursday

Friday

Saturday

Sunday

Reflections

Colour Me In

Soothing

Soothing

It's not often that we consider what we could do to soothe ourselves. As women and mothers we are often soothing our babies or children or encouraging our work colleagues,friends and family, while our own needs can be pushed to the side.

Take some time this month to consider what you find soothing, maybe it's soaking your feet in warm water, having a spa, going for a massage, enjoying a new herbal tea or taking some time in the day to lie down, close your eyes and listen to some soothing music.

" Rest and self care are so important, when you take the time to replenish your spirit it allows you to serve others from the overflow. You cannot serve from an empty vessel."

-Eleanor Brown-

Important Projects

Where you get to focus on the important over the urgent

Think About...	Work on...	Finished!

My three main intentions for this month:

One	Two	Three

Could do list

_____

_____

_____

_____

_____

_____

_____

_____

_____

_____

_____

_____

_____

_____

"Very little is needed to make a happy life"

- Unknown -

This Month

Monday	Tuesday	Wednesday	Thursday

Get Creative...
Bake a new recipe, trying out something new is fun and you get to share and enjoy the creation at the end.

Friday	Saturday	Sunday

Notes and Scribbles

Soothing

Soothing

"The body benefits from movement and the mind benefits from stillness"
- Saleyong Miphem -

Monday
_____

Tuesday
_____

Wednesday
_____

Thursday

Friday

Saturday

Sunday

Soothing

"A little thing, like children putting flowers in my hair,
can fill up the widening cracks in my self-assurance like soothing lanolin."
-Sylvia Plath-

Monday

Tuesday

Wednesday

Thursday

Friday

Saturday

Sunday

Soothing

"Children crave routine and find listening to the same stories over and over again soothing. If you've grown weary of the holiday books you've read your kid 7,883 times, try adding 'dude' to the end of every line of dialogue."
-Adam Mansbach-

Monday

Tuesday

Wednesday

Thursday

Friday

Saturday

Sunday

Soothing

"The planet does not need more "successful people". The planet desperately
needs more peacemakers, healers, restorers, storytellers and lovers of all kinds."
- Dalai Lama -

Monday
_____

Tuesday
_____

Wednesday
_____

Thursday

Friday

Saturday

Sunday

Soothing

*"Do your little bit of good where you are, it's those
little bits of good put together that overwhelm the world"
- Desmond Tutu -*

Monday

Tuesday

Wednesday

Thursday

Friday

Saturday

Sunday

Reflections

Colour Me In

H. D. L. CORBY

crotalarioid nodules predominant Most legumes that produce
iatic nodules show some tendency in their nodules towards

Pleasant

Pleasant

What a myriad of things are pleasant in our world if we give our time and attention to them. The warm sun on your back, a gentle walk along the seashore, a yummy meal shared with a friend or loved one.

The smell of a freshly cut rose, the aroma of a steaming cup of coffee and the comfort of a warm hug.

How delightfully pleasing.

" Wander often, Wonder always."

- Unknown-

Important Projects

Where you get to focus on the important over the urgent

Think About...	Work on...	Finished!

My three main intentions for this month:

One	Two	Three

Could do list

_____

_____

_____

_____

_____

_____

_____

_____

_____

_____

_____

_____

_____

_____

"Be pleasant until ten o'clock
in the morning and the rest of the day will take care of itself."

-Elbert Hubbard-

Pleasant

Monday	Tuesday	Wednesday	Thursday

Get Creative...
Buy yourself a simple sketch book and some softer pencils such as 2B and 6B pencils.
Head out into nature and find small objects to sketch such as leaves, feathers or flowers.
Anything that takes your fancy. Or, search up the many 30 day sketchbook challenges to
give you some ideas on different things to sketch. Mix things up by cutting our magazine
pictures that you like to glue into your sketchbook or words/quotes you find inspiring.
Colouring in crayons are lovely to add some colour too! Start simple and your confidence
will grow.

"There is perhaps no solitary sensation so exquisite as that of slumbering on the grass or hay, shaded from the hot sun by a tree, with the consciousness of a fresh light air running through the wide atmosphere and the sky stretching far overhead upon all sides." -Leigh Hunt-

Friday	Saturday	Sunday

Notes and Scribbles

Pleasant

Pleasant

"Have regular hours for work and play; make each day both useful and pleasant, and prove that you understand the worth of time by employing it well. Then youth will be delightful, old age will bring few regrets, and life will become a beautiful success." –Louisa May Alcott–

Monday
_____

Tuesday
_____

Wednesday
_____

Thursday

Friday

Saturday

Sunday

Pleasant

"Arranging a bowl of flowers in the morning can give a sense of quiet in a crowded day, like writing a poem or saying a prayer"
- Anne Morrow Lindbergh -

Monday

Tuesday

Wednesday

Thursday

Friday

Saturday

Sunday

Pleasant

"And so while others miserably pledge themselves to the insatiable pursuit of ambition and brief power, I will be stretched out in the shade singing."
-Fray Luis De Leon-

Monday

Tuesday

Wednesday

Thursday

Friday

Saturday

Sunday

Pleasant

"Happiness is a butterfly, which, when pursued, is always just beyond your grasp;
but which, if you will sit down quietly, may come and alight on you."
- Nathaniel Hawthorne -

Monday

Tuesday

Wednesday

Thursday

Friday

Saturday

Sunday

Pleasant

"Today's little moments become tomorrows precious memories"
- Unknown -

Monday
_____

Tuesday
_____

Wednesday
_____

Thursday

Friday

Saturday

Sunday

Reflections

Colour Me In

H. D. L. Corby

AYANA, H. S., AND GOTHWAL, B. D. (1964). A contribution to the
root nodules in some legumes. *Proc. Indian Acad. Sci.*, **59**, 350–
EN, I. (1981). Ingeae. In: *Advances in Legume Systematics* ed. R.
nd P. H. Raven. Royal Botanic Gardens, London.
s, D. O. (1956). Legumes and their symbiosis
gric., **24**, 247–270.
s, D. O. (1969). Observations on the nodulation status of
eguminous species in Amazonia and Guiana. *Trop. Agric., Trini*
45–151.
DINY-MIECZYNSKA. A. (1949). Studies on the root nodules of l
lants. *Bull. Int. Acad. Polon. Sci., Cl. Sci. Math. Ser. B-1*,
3–83.
HURST, C. E., AND SPRENT, J. I. (1975). Surface features of soyl
odules. *Protoplasma*, **85**, 85–98
J. S. (1961). Perennial nodules on native legumes in the Brit
Nature, **192**, 376–377.

Content

Content

Too often in life we lose our peace because we are not content with our daily lives. We have a tendency to focus too much on what we don't have and in our struggle to reach our goals and dreams, we lose sight of where we have come from and all that we do have, have achieved and been blessed with!

Keep the Bigger picture in mind. Look at your life from the outside in occasionally, and tune into all that you do have and hold and get to experience. Your life is someone else's dream.

"Be happy with what you have while working for what you want."

- Unknown-

Important Projects

Where you get to focus on the important over the urgent

Think About...	Work on...	Finished!

My three main intentions for this month:

One	Two	Three

Could do list

"He is richest who is content with the least, for content is the wealth of nature."

-Socrates-

This Month

Monday	Tuesday	Wednesday	Thursday

Get Creative...
Read a book of poetry.

"My crown is called content, a crown that seldom kings enjoy."

-William Shakespeare-

Friday	Saturday	Sunday

Notes and Scribbles

Content

Content

"When you are content to be simply yourself
and don't compare or compete, everybody will respect you."
-Lao Tzu-

Monday
_____

Tuesday
_____

Wednesday
_____

Thursday

Friday

Saturday

Sunday

Content

"You are rich when you are content and happy with what you have"
- Unknown -

Monday

Tuesday

Wednesday

Thursday

Friday

Saturday

Sunday

Content

"There's no happier person than a truly thankful, content person."
- Joyce Meyer-

Monday

Tuesday

Wednesday

Thursday

Friday

Saturday

Sunday

Content

"Happiness is not having what you want. It is appreciating what you have"
- Unknown -

Monday
_____

Tuesday
_____

Wednesday
_____

Thursday

Friday

Saturday

Sunday

Content

"To pray is to walk in the full light of God, and to say simply, without holding back, I am human and you are God"
- Philip Yancey -

Monday
_____

Tuesday
_____

Wednesday
_____

Thursday

Friday

Saturday

Sunday

Reflections

Colour Me In

Cosy

Classification	No. species reportedly nodulating	Nodule size (mm×10⁻¹) axial×trans.	Descriptive code	Reference No.	Comments
Desmanthus	3			4	
D. illinoensis		88× 25	422 C		
D. virgatus		50× 20	422 C		
D. virgatus		146× 28	422 C		
D. virgatus		108× 25	422 C		
D. virgatus		132× 27	422 C	24	Fig. 11. Also Fig.
D. virgatus		100× 25	422 C		
Dichrostachys	2			4	
D. cinerea		73× 25	422 C		
D. cinerea		62× 22	422 C		

Cosy

Take some time to get cosy and comfy this month. Indulge in some PJ days, get lost in a good book or a movie. Get yourself a soft new cuddle blanket and a hot water bottle.

My favourite is putting on my soft socks before putting my feet up on the couch in the evening.

"To be soft is to be powerful"

-Rupi Kaur, Milk and Honey-

Important Projects

Where you get to focus on the important over the urgent

Think About...	Work on...	Finished!

My three main intentions for this month:

One	Two	Three

Could do list

_____
_____
_____
_____
_____
_____
_____
_____
_____
_____
_____
_____
_____
_____
_____
_____
_____

"I am a big fan of cosy. I get very excited by a roaring fire and even a perfectly made cup of tea. And being married really is the ultimate in cosy, so I couldn't be more content."

-Sophie Winkleman-

Cosy

Monday	Tuesday	Wednesday	Thursday

Get Creative...
Join a creative community group such as a painting or drawing class, a quilting group, or a photography group.

"I like cosy, intimate houses."

-Tori Amos-

Friday	Saturday	Sunday

Notes and Scribbles

Cosy

Cosy

"Hold onto whatever keeps you warm inside"
- Unknown -

Monday

Tuesday

Wednesday

Thursday
_____

Friday
_____

Saturday
_____

Sunday
_____

Cosy

"I don't have one favourite spot – I love writing anywhere that I feel inspired. I have to admit that I do love getting cosy in bed or under blankets on the sofa and writing from there."
-Ella Woodward-

Monday

Tuesday

Wednesday

Thursday

Friday

Saturday

Sunday

Cosy

"Routines may include taking a warm bath or a relaxing walk in the evening, or practicing meditation/relaxation exercises. Psychologically, the completion of such a practice tells your mind and body that the day's work is over and you are free to relax and sleep." -Andrew Weil-

Monday
_____

Tuesday
_____

Wednesday
_____

Thursday

Friday

Saturday

Sunday

Cosy

"The perfect antidote to dark, cold and creepy is light, warm and cosy".
-Candice Olson-

Monday

Tuesday

Wednesday

Thursday

Friday

Saturday

Sunday

Cosy

"What feeling is so nice as a child's hand in yours?
So small, so soft and warm, like a kitten huddling in the shelter of your clasp."
-Marjorie Holmes-

Monday
_____

Tuesday
_____

Wednesday
_____

Thursday

Friday

Saturday

Sunday

Reflections

Colour Me In

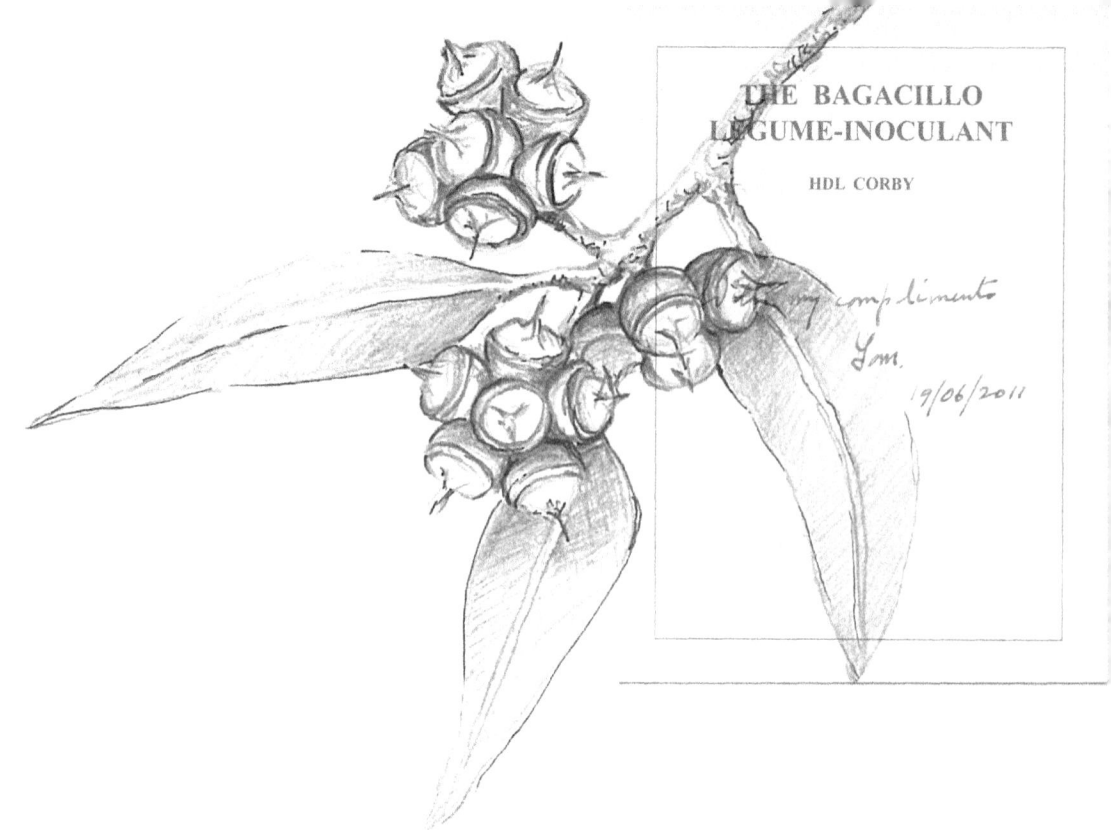

THE BAGACILLO
LEGUME-INOCULANT

HDL CORBY

my compliments

Ym.

19/06/2011

Tranquil

Tranquil

Being out in nature is a wonderful soother for the soul.
There's something calming about all the green and blue colours.
Plan to spend some time in the tranquil surroundings of a beautiful
garden, forest, park, riverside or beach.

Take in the colours, sounds and scents.

"The rest notes in the music of our lives are the places that
bring the greatest beauty."

-Amanda Viviers-

Important Projects

Where you get to focus on the important over the urgent

Think About...	Work on...	Finished!

My three main intentions for this month:

One	Two	Three

Could do list

"The more tranquil a man becomes, the greater is his success, his influence, his power for good. Calmness of mind is one of the beautiful jewels of wisdom."

-James Allen-

This Month

Monday	Tuesday	Wednesday	Thursday

Get Creative...
Create a meaningful scrapbook album for a loved one or as a memory book for yourself.

"The pursuit, even of the best things, ought to be calm and tranquil."

-Marcus Tullius Cicero-

Friday	Saturday	Sunday

Notes and Scribbles

Tranquil

Tranquil

Monday

Tuesday

Wednesday

Thursday

Friday

Saturday

Sunday

Tranquil

"Gratitude changes the pangs of memory into a tranquil joy."
-Dietrich Bonhoeffer-

Monday

Tuesday

Wednesday

Thursday

Friday

Saturday

Sunday

Tranquil

"It is neither wealth nor splendor;
but tranquility and occupation which give you happiness."
-Thomas Jefferson-

Monday

Tuesday

Wednesday

Thursday

Friday

Saturday

Sunday

Tranquil

"I see the world being slowly transformed into a wilderness; I hear the approaching thunder that, one day, will destroy us too. I feel the suffering of millions. And yet, when I look up at the sky, I somehow feel that everything will change for the better, that this cruelty too shall end, that peace and tranquility will return once more." -Anne Frank-

Monday

Tuesday

Wednesday

Thursday

Friday

Saturday

Sunday

Tranquil

"Today I choose calm over chaos, serenity over stress, peace over perfection,
grace over grit and faith over fear"
- Mary Davis -

Monday

Tuesday

Wednesday

Thursday

Friday

Saturday

Sunday

Reflections

Colour Me In

Retreat

POSTSCRIPT

Since my day, the Netherlands Government has funded a
...ement of the original mud-brick Factory and Laboratory;
...l Seeds Producers' Association has funded a replacement of
...ctory's worn equipment; the International Monetary Fund
...ed Dr Paul Davis for a three week stint as resident Consulta...
...biologist; bagacillo has been replaced by finer hammer-
...bagasse; the Factory has come under the wing of the Soil
...tivity Research Laboratory, and is in charge of Joram...

Retreats

Set aside some time to have your own personal "retreat" or maybe plan to go on one with a few friends. It's an opportunity to withdraw from the busy busy of your everyday.

It's a great opportunity to reflect, ponder and tweak things in your life. A wonderful way to get a fresh perspective.

"Some days the world is too loud for a quiet soul."

-J.Rose-

Important Projects

Where you get to focus on the important over the urgent

Think About...	Work on...	Finished!

My three main intentions for this month:

One	Two	Three

Could do list

_____

_____

_____

_____

_____

_____

_____

_____

_____

_____

_____

_____

_____

_____

"Come away with me to a quiet place and rest awhile"

- Mark 6:31-

This Month

Monday	Tuesday	Wednesday	Thursday

Get Creative...
Plan a storytelling night around a winter fire with family or friends, either sharing old family stories or reading a book together.

"That perfect tranquillity of life, which is nowhere to be found but in retreat,
a faithful friend and a good library."

-Aphra Behn-

Friday	Saturday	Sunday

Notes and Scribbles

Retreatr

Retreat

"It's no coincidence that the word 'holiday' suggests a holy day, or that the longest book in the Torah concerns the Sabbath. If you wish to advance in any sphere, the best way is to take a retreat"
-Pico Iyer-

Monday

Tuesday

Wednesday

Thursday

Friday

Saturday

Sunday

Retreat

"Cows are my passion. What I have ever sighed for has been
to retreat to a Swiss farm, and live entirely surrounded by cows - and china."
-Charles Dickens-

Monday
_____

Tuesday
_____

Wednesday
_____

Thursday

Friday

Saturday

Sunday

Retreat

"In my college years, I would retreat to our summer house for two weeks in June to read a novel a day. How exciting it was, after pouring my coffee and making myself comfortable on the porch, to open the next book on the roster, read the first sentences, and find myself on the platform of a train station."
-Amor Towles-

Monday

Tuesday

Wednesday

Thursday

Friday

Saturday

Sunday

Retreat

"Writing books is a nice retreat. There's nothing quite like diving into a book for a few hours. That is a big time vacation."
-Padgett Powell-

Monday
_____

Tuesday
_____

Wednesday
_____

Thursday

Friday

Saturday

Sunday

Retreat

"We need to find God, and he cannot be found in noise and restlessness. God is the friend of silence. See how nature - trees, flowers, grass- grows in silence; see the stars, the moon and the sun, how they move in silence... We need silence to be able to touch souls"
-Mother Teresa-

Monday
_____

Tuesday
_____

Wednesday
_____

Thursday

Friday

Saturday

Sunday

Reflections

Colour Me In

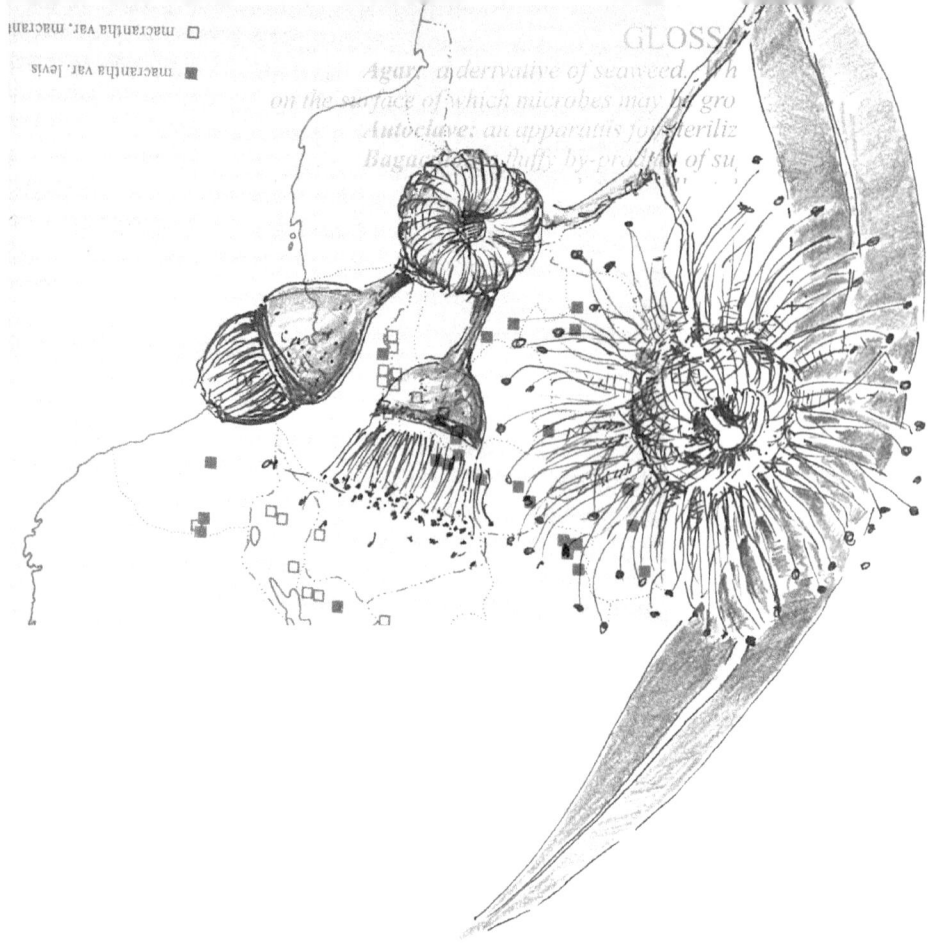

Laughter

Laughter

Laughter is a gift that we should indulge in more often than we do!
The therapeutic benefits of laughter are endless ! Seek to find the
humour in your everyday life. Don't take life too seriously.

Laughter has been described as one of the best natural
tranquilizers in the world, its a sure path to feeling more
happy and peaceful.

"A day without laughter is a day wasted."
-Charlie Chaplin-

Important Projects

Where you get to focus on the important over the urgent

Think About...	Work on...	Finished!

My three main intentions for this month:

One	Two	Three

Could do list

_____
_____
_____
_____
_____
_____
_____
_____
_____
_____
_____
_____
_____
_____
_____
_____

"Laughter is an instant vacation."

-Milton Berle-

This Month

Monday	Tuesday	Wednesday	Thursday
	Get Creative... Do some gardening. Grow something from seeds, or plant up a herb garden or some spring bulbs.		

"To me there is no picture so beautiful as smiling, bright-eyed, happy children; no music so sweet as their clear and ringing laughter."

-P. T. Barnum-

Friday	Saturday	Sunday

Notes and Scribbles

Laughter

Laughter

"Feelings aroused by the touch of someone's hand, the sound of music,
the smell of a flower, a beautiful sunset, a work of art, love, laughter, hope and
faith –all work on both the unconscious and the conscious
aspects of the self, and they have physiological consequences as well".
–Bernie Siegel–

Monday

Tuesday

Wednesday

Thursday

Friday

Saturday

Sunday

Laughter

"The person who can bring the spirit of laughter into a room is indeed blessed"
-Bennett Cerf-

Monday
_____

Tuesday
_____

Wednesday
_____

Thursday

Friday

Saturday

Sunday

Laughter

"Hearty laughter is a good way to jog internally without having to go outdoors"
-Norman Cousins-

Monday

Tuesday

Wednesday

Thursday

Friday

Saturday

Sunday

Laughter

"Laughter is important, not only because it makes us happy,
it also has actual health benefits. And that's because laughter completely
engages the body and releases the mind. It connects us to others, and that in itself
has a healing effect" -Marlo Thomas-

Monday

Tuesday

Thursday

Friday

Saturday

Sunday

Laughter

"Laughter is a tranquilizer with no side effects"
-Arnold H. Glasow-

Monday

Tuesday

Wednesday

Thursday

Friday

Saturday

Sunday

Reflections

Laughter

Colour Me In

Restful

No. recognized genera[1]	No. known species[1]	No. genera reportedly forming	No. genera reportedly lacking	No. species reportedly forming	No. species reportedly lacking	No. genera with known nodule	No. species with known nodule	Oblate	Basic nodule sha... 2	3	4	Girdling	Cylindric
25	250	3	6	4	13	0	0	—	—				
47	360	8	13	10	42	2	3	2					
20	600	4	3	48	49	3	18	—	—				
5	260	1	1	1	32	0	3	—	—				
55	455	11	10	12	31	3	3	1					
2	1 200	2	0	195	10	2	57	—					
21	990	13	0	78	8	10	32	—					
37	750	15	4	59	14	11	29	—					
1	1	0	2	0	0	1	0	—					
2	40	0	0	5	1	0	1	—					
1	15	1	0	5	0	1		5					

Restful

Find those things that switch you into a restful state, it is one of the most undervalued gifts we all need. Our society and culture seems to associate being restful with laziness.

The truth is quite the opposite, as when we rest we are more productive, happy and healthy.

"Take a rest. A field that has rested gives a beautiful crop."

-Ovid-

Important Projects

Where you get to focus on the important over the urgent

Think About...	Work on...	Finished!

My three main intentions for this month:

One	Two	Three

Could do list

_____

_____

_____

_____

_____

_____

_____

_____

_____

_____

_____

_____

_____

_____

"A cat pours his body on the floor like water. It is restful just to see him."

-William Lyon Phelps-

This Month

Monday	Tuesday	Wednesday	Thursday

Get Creative...
Go and visit an Art Gallery

"Restful sleep is a key ingredient to living a miraculous life. I'm not saying we need eight or ten hours a night to feel fully rested. In fact, sometimes less sleep can be more restorative than many hours. The key is to have real sleep... the drooling-on-the-pillow kind of sleep"

-Gabrielle Bernstein-

Friday	Saturday	Sunday

Notes and Scribbles

Restful

Restful

"Rest is not idleness, and to lie sometimes on the grass under trees on a summer's day, listening to the murmur of the water, or watching the clouds float across the sky, is by no means a waste of time"
- John Lubbock-

Monday

Tuesday

Wednesday

Thursday

Friday

Saturday

Sunday

Restful

"There is virtue in work and there is virtue in rest. Use both and overlook neither."
- Alan Cohen -

Monday

Tuesday

Wednesday

Thursday

Friday

Saturday

Sunday

Restful

"Sleeping is like meditation:
it's good to rest the body but also to shut the mind down for a bit"
-Anthony Joshua-

Monday
_____

Tuesday
_____

Wednesday
_____

Thursday

Friday

Saturday

Sunday

Restful

"My idea of Heaven is to wake up,
have a good breakfast, and spend the rest of the day drawing"
-Peter Falk-

Monday

Tuesday

Wednesday

Thursday

Friday

Saturday

Sunday

Restful

"I just want to say, good night, sweet prince, may flights of angels sing thee to thy rest"
-Harry Dean Stanton-

Monday

Tuesday

Wednesday

Thursday

Friday

Saturday

Sunday

Reflections

Colour Me In

Surrender

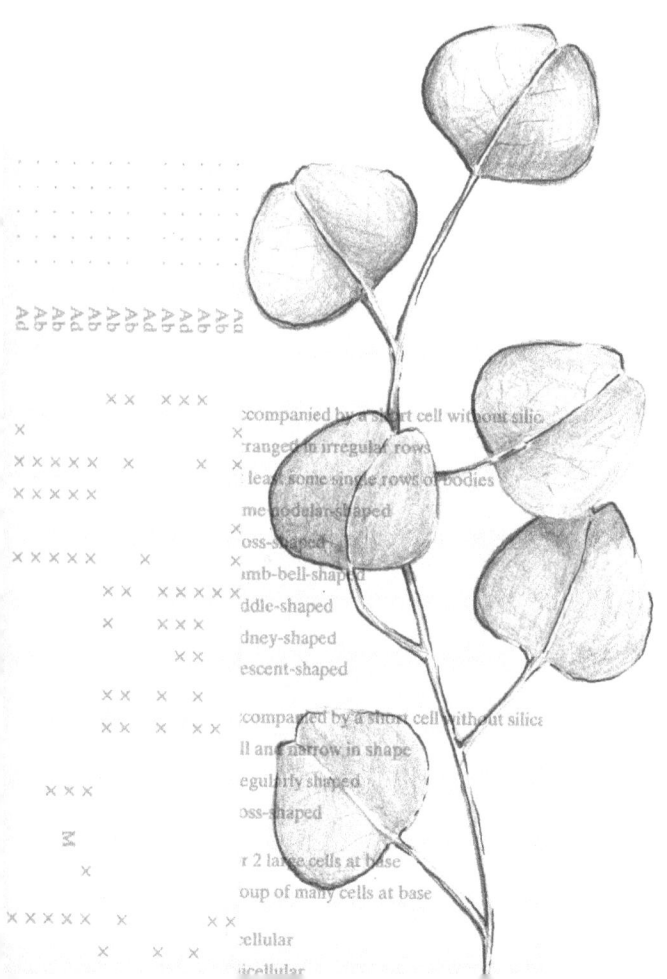

accompanied by a short cell without silica
arranged in irregular rows
at least some single rows of bodies
some nodular-shaped
cross-shaped
dumb-bell-shaped
saddle-shaped
kidney-shaped
crescent-shaped

accompanied by a short cell without silica
small and narrow in shape
irregularly shaped
cross-shaped

or 2 large cells at base
group of many cells at base

unicellular
multicellular

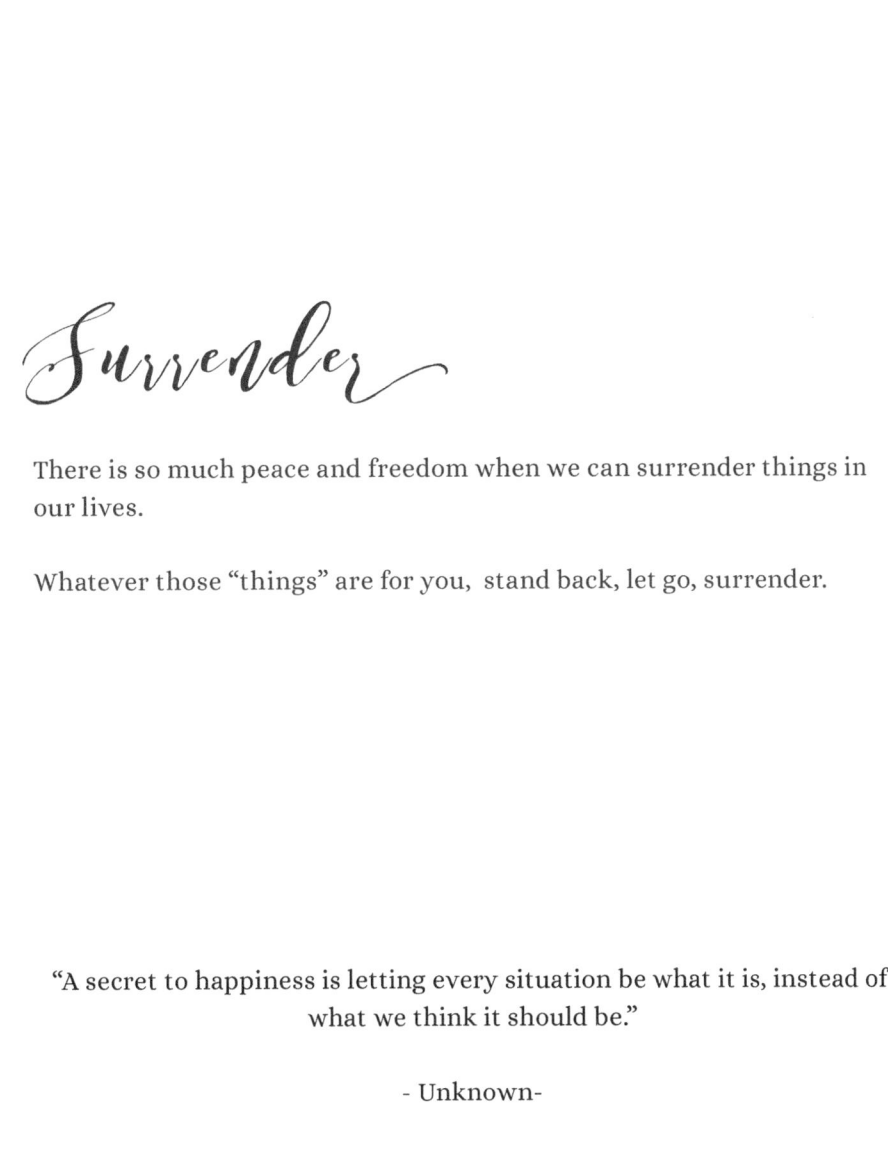

Surrender

There is so much peace and freedom when we can surrender things in our lives.

Whatever those "things" are for you, stand back, let go, surrender.

"A secret to happiness is letting every situation be what it is, instead of what we think it should be."

- Unknown-

Important Projects

Where you get to focus on the important over the urgent

Think About...	Work on...	Finished!

My three main intentions for this month:

One	Two	Three

Could do list

_____

_____

_____

_____

_____

_____

_____

_____

_____

_____

_____

_____

_____

_____

"Prayer is an altar for surrender. A place we go to hand everything over to God."

-Margaret Feinberg-

This Month

Monday	Tuesday	Wednesday	Thursday

Get Creative...
Create a Pintrest account, you'll be blown away by the creative inspiration.

"Research has shown that time pressure leads to tunnel vision and that people think more creatively when they are calm, unhurried and free from stress and distractions. We all know this from experience"

-Carl Honore-

Friday	Saturday	Sunday

Notes and Scribbles

Surrender

Surrender

"If you surrender completely to the moments
as they pass, you live more richly those moments"
-Anne Morrow Lindbergh-

Monday

Tuesday

Wednesday

Thursday

Friday

Saturday

Sunday

Surrender

"The creative process is a process of surrender, not control"
-Julia Cameron-

Monday
_____

Tuesday
_____

Wednesday
_____

Thursday

Friday

Saturday

Sunday

Surrender

"I've been praying that we might have a spiritual awakening. But I think that becomes possible as individuals surrender their lives fresh and anew to Christ"
-Billy Graham-

Monday

Tuesday

Wednesday

Thursday

Friday

Saturday

Sunday

Surrender

"The greatness of a man's power is the measure of his surrender"
-William Booth-

Monday

Tuesday

Wednesday

Thursday

Friday

Saturday

Sunday

Surrender

"Sometimes renewal comes in surrender"
- Ros Bell -

Monday
_____

Tuesday
_____

Wednesday
_____

Thursday

Friday

Saturday

Sunday

Reflections

Colour Me In

Comforting

Comforting

Embrace the joy of the Christmas and Holiday season.
Take comfort in the company of your loved ones,

It's time to celebrate, give thanks and relax.
May this be your most Peaceful Christmas yet!

"Find Comfort in the Chaos."

- Unknown-

Important Projects

Where you get to focus on the important over the urgent

Think About...	Work on...	Finished!

My three main intentions for this month:

One	Two	Three

Could do list

_____

_____

_____

_____

_____

_____

_____

_____

_____

_____

_____

_____

_____

_____

"Expect trouble as an inevitable part of life and repeat to yourself, the most comforting words of all; this, too, shall pass."

-Ann Landers-

This Month

Monday	Tuesday	Wednesday	Thursday
		Get Creative... Go to the theatre or a musical evening..	

"It's so comforting to have a small piece of cake. Just one slice"

-Mary Berry-

Friday	Saturday	Sunday

Notes and Scribbles

Comforting

Comforting

"Baking cookies is comforting, and cookies are
the sweetest little bit of comfort food. They are very bite-sized and personal"
- Sandra Lee-

Monday

Tuesday

Wednesday

Thursday

Friday

Saturday

Sunday

Comforting

"Sometimes you meet a person and you just click. You're comfortable with them and you don't have to pretend to be anyone or anything"
- Unknown -

Monday
_____

Tuesday
_____

Wednesday
_____

Thursday

Friday

Saturday

Sunday

Comforting

"Celebrate every victory"
- Unknown -

Monday

Tuesday

Wednesday

Thursday

Friday

Saturday

Sunday

Comforting

"Having your house fill up with the people you love is comforting"
-Sheryl Sandberg-

Monday
_____

Tuesday
_____

Wednesday
_____

Thursday

Friday

Saturday

Sunday

Comforting

"Silent night, holy night. All is calm, all is bright"
- Silent Night -

Monday

Tuesday

Wednesday

Thursday

Friday

Saturday

Sunday

Reflections

Colour Me In

Dedications

As my sales grow, I would love to donate a portion of my profits to the Not for Profit *Foundations for Farming* Zimbabwe, aimed at bringing transformation to individuals, communities and nations through faithful and productive use of land using a simple but fruitful conservation farming method.

www.foundationsforfarming.org

Thank you

To my dearest family
Derek for your unconditional love and support
For our many laughs together
For having my back always
Even in the darkest night
Rachel, Nicole and Judah
For being the best gifts from God I always hoped for
For being my biggest teachers
My precious chickens
You have made my cup overflow
I love you all up to the moon
And BIG as the sky
And DEEP as the Bunker
Grateful THANKS to Katie Bullied who birthed this vision with me

Text Copyright © Ashleigh Vincent 2018.
Illustration Copyright © Ashleigh Vincent
Design Work and Layout © Alexandria Davis & Kate Stagg from Parklife Group Pty Ltd
Cover Design © Kate Stagg from Parklife Group Pty Ltd
Grateful thanks to Publisher Karen McDermott

First published in Australia 2018 by Karen McDermott
www.karenmcdermott.com.au

National Library of Australia Cataloguing-in-Publisher data:
Non-fiction- planner.

ISBN 978-0-6483850-0-4

Lightning Source UK Ltd.
Milton Keynes UK
UKHW051017250820
368786UK00003B/40